EDGES

Philip Lawder

Printed and bound in the UK

ISBN 978-1-291-51363-9

For Jeannine, with love and gratitude

CONTENTS

COME, SIT WITH ME

Come, sit with me
but let's not talk,
just watch the swifts in evening waltz.
I'll touch your hand as the sagging sun
gives up his day to our night.
You'll dream my dreams and I'll dream yours,
deep, delving deep in the liquid dark.

Not for us the midnight manic muse
that elsewhere dances,
skittering in the half-assembled mind
of the bloating banker, counting stars like coins,
or the tottering drunk, roaring like a steam train
through the wreckage of a half-remembered song.

Ours is an altogether softer muse
that settles on shoulders like a forgotten shawl,
takes the detritus of downtrodden hopes
in its gentle potter's hands,
shaping and forming until, reburnished,
new hope for old ascends
and we, with it, once again
are gods.

TOO FAR AWAY

'Hope to see you some time this year',
scribbled in haste in the Christmas card.
Casual gesture, and so well intended,
you were always
too far away.

Families grew, the years passed fast,
stretching away from those childhood fields,
hide and seek in the woods, never could be found.
Always
too far away

Casual snog at the teenage dance,
when all other options had crashed and burned.
Lips connect, nothing else, glazed eyes looking round
you were always
too far away

Then I heard of your vicious invader
'Of course I'll come down, as soon as I'm free,'
but I hemmed myself in with important things
and you were always
too far away

In that last chat, could tell it had won,
could hear, down deep, your last curtain call.
We were close as we talked, many memories shared,
not quite
so far away.

Now, in the silence, we're talking again,
your rumbling chuckle, non-sequitor chat.
Though I never quite made it, forgive me, you see,
you were always
too far away.

MY GRANDFATHER'S STUDY

The clock tock-tocks imperiously,
breaking silence with its warning.
Glass-front bookcase, overflowing,
challenges.

Stranded on the roll-top desk
on yellow paper, copper plate
from fountain pen and Quink Royal Blue
circles out next Sunday's sermon,
incomplete.

And, planted in this magic place
in black and white on swivel chair,
my grandfather
twinkles down through wire-rimmed glasses,
holds out hands like gnarled old oak
and waits.

But I hold the soft aroma,
Polished wood and leathered books
blending with the dust protected
in this dark, male sanctuary.
It is the smell of time and contemplation
of faith embedded, interwoven,
whole.

And I, short-trousered, Aertex-shirted,
bare feet tickled by the carpet,
hope that I can stay forever,
know that I shall miss it
every day.

ON FROGATT EDGE

Frowning down like the angry parent
on the tamed fields and skittering road,
the high rock stands, black as time,
scarred and fissured by the enemy wind.

And you and I, who clambered insolent
onto the giant's head,
rattled by the wind,
billowed by joy,
see across the zigzag of the dry stone walls
tonight's rain, crouching like an ambush,
behind the distant, lowering hill,

see the small town huddled far below,
begging permission from the guardian peaks.
Shy wisps of smoke
promise apple pies and thick, dark tea
but we, the climbers of the kingdom,
stay.

You turn to me
cheeks red and eyes on fire.
Across the wind you call
love's three unchanging words.

And I reply, yet in my cleverness
cannot leave well alone, must
qualify, explain and modify.
And with my wandering words and shifting eye
the glory shatters
and we’re just on a hill on a cold damp day.

THE IMMIGRANT BOY

He stands and he gazes and tries not to think
of the homes these people will go to,
of the colours and sounds and smells that he's left,
of the old men that he can't say no to.

Queuing in Starbucks for what they call coffee,
they ask him his name and he lies.
Knowing they'll never unravel his syllables,
knowing the look that will burn in their eyes.

Around him this cold weather language is spoken
without moving lips, arms or heart.
It dribbles about him like water on pebbles,
its sibilants tearing the stranger apart.

To him every word just sounds like an insult,
an accusation or threat
that will send him back home, alone and defeated
by ignorance, prejudice, hatred and debt.

He touches the letter that sits in his pocket,
looks out at the sorrowing day
that is closing, half-hearted, beyond misted windows;
promises drifting to black from dark grey

And he knows why he came and he knows it's not true;
these streets are not paved with gold.
And the one thing he's learnt in this desolate town,
the thing that ensures that he will stay down:
he's invisible, has-been at eighteen years old.

SUPERMARKET, THURSDAY MORNING

Old men seem surprised by the onslaught of age
as if, one day, they'd come back
from nature's all too frequent call
to find a young usurper
sitting at their desk,
answering their phone,
and their coat and briefcase stacked outside the door.

Where once they guided ships of state
now they guide a trolley,
bewildered at events that turn,
unpredicted as the trolley's wheels.
Now, marooned, these men take their orders,
scurrying like spaniels to find the cheapest soup,
proud to spot a discount on the chops.

Their wives look on, exasperated,
their fiefdom now usurped
by these, their role-less spouses wanting lunch.
Once a reason to boast,
'My husband the surgeon, the lawyer, the boss,'
now 'Oh him, yes, he's here',
whenever the girls come round.

Less use than a machine
less loveable than a pet,
pushed off to the pub, the cricket or the garden,
now, like age itself,
he’s just spoiling her fun.

SCATTERED SHOWERS

Rain.
Again.
Here it comes, busy-bodying
along the straggling promenade,
scurrying bathers into steamy cafés
where they sit and drip and sip their tannin teas.

Father thinks of the journey home,
bumper to bumper, temper to temper
chauffeuring squabbling kids and silent wife
through unnoticed splendour of the twilight downs.

Mother thinks of the burger boy's smile,
the lifeguard's shoulders and the waiter's bum.
The sun's brief touch has wakened sleeping dreams;
they'll be buried under chores before Redhill.

The kids punch buttons, twiddle knobs,
exterminate thousands as their ice cream thaws
and drips on their knees, where it blends with the sand
soothing red skin from a hurried Brighton sun.

And the rain beats on the window
like an angry landlord,
impatient, seeing the approaching blue,
demanding payment for a summer's day.

TIME

Has anyone got my time?
I seem to have mislaid it
somewhere between the Sainsbury's shop
and the delays on the Northern Line.

I can remember, but only just,
How, like drunken gamblers, we'd squander the hours,
wander by river, lie long in bed
watch the shadows mark the passing,
discarding each day like a crumpled tissue,
Our pockets full of so many more.

Has anyone seen my life?
I'm sure I left it here somewhere,
tucked between the deadline and the mortgage.
Thank God for those wasted hours.

A SANDWICH IN HOLBORN

It's a polite, tidy sandwich,
impeccably sliced,
compiled,
accurate to the gram,
not a crumb out of place.
Cosy in its plastic carapace,
it proclaims in twenty point Helvetica
its promise of ultimate pleasure.
Avocado, tomato, mozzarella; vowel-ending, vivid words
carrying the faintest scent of sunshine
out to this cold, grey place.

I wander,
harried by snarling buildings,
blind-eyed, storeyed windows,
Saturday abandoned.
And there, a tree,
well, nearly a tree,
crouching against the side of a house
like a forgotten refugee;
I can almost hear it cough.
But it reaches up,
sap-deep bonding with the sun.
And in that longing stretch,
its random, hopeful shapes

shame the harsh rectangles that surround it
like bullies in the playground.

A reminder.
It was not always so,
and this solidity,
embarrassed brick and arrogant concrete,
will pass like the rest of us.
So much has passed before,
layer upon layer,
back to a time when,
from this low hill,
we would have watched the river flow,
unfettered and unschooled,
running with a child's pure joy,
oblivious of the finite.

No avocados then,
wheat harvested fast,
fearful of marauders,
then stored against the winter's unblocked blast.
And, to the East, the bedraggled city
whose smell, when the wind blew,
would carry with it death and defecation.

London has moved on from that frightened child,
through vigorous youth,
complacent middle age,
to become this sluggish, bloated painted lady,

not knowing how she got here,
retelling the same old stories
to anyone who'll listen
of long-forgotten loves and triumphs
and fearful of the future.

And in this small corner on this cold damp day,
it's just me and a sandwich.
Tomato, avocado, mozzarella.
It's good, but, in the end, it's just a sandwich.

INCIDENT AT TESCO'S

Last Thursday at 4.32
between the cat food and the packs of Typhoo
in Tesco's superstore,
I started to dance, with the air,
just a simple waltz round the black and white squares
of the partly polished floor.

Lilian Reilly née Porter
widow of Bath, visiting her daughter,
paused by the honey and jam.
Quite bold for a former schoolma'am,
abandoning trolley, she held out her arm
I asked 'Are you dancing?' 'I am'.

Well, we chasséed and sidestepped with style
past cornflakes and kitchen towels, pile upon pile,
right up to the manager's door.
'Turn up the music,' we cried
but our request was brutally, flatly denied.
Said Lil, 'That man is a bore.'

So, she curtsied, I bowed, unconvinced.
I went back to my biscuits, she to her mince,
back to whoever we are.
But Lil, we must do this some more
by the shampoos, tomorrow, round about four?
We can practise our cha cha cha.

HOME AND AWAY

When you went back to live with your mother,
Strictly Come Dancing glittered
and swirled on other people's screens,
usurped on ours, on mine, by rugby
and raucous late night laughs.

When you went back to live with your mother,
the vegetables in the fridge
crouched in their keep-fresh compartment.
Entombed, ignored, they huddled together,
hugging remnants of sun.

When you went back to live with your mother,
newspapers gathered in every corner,
whispering gobbets of scandalous news.
The 'I must get round to it' pile
flowed over like Etna,
your To Do list fluttered to the floor
and the ironing basket sulked.

When you went back to live with your mother,
the bed grew to the size of Wembley,
cold as a station platform, dull as a Maths exam.

And, though the heating was perfect,
the meals acceptably greasy
and the beer cans stood proud on your art nouveau cabinet,
I felt like a foreigner.

When you came back from your mother,
we argued.

SUBURBAN SONG

Sometimes I imagine dancing on ceilings,
spinning and cartwheels, stomping and jive.
I suppose such an action might bolster my feelings,
give more of a sense of being alive.

Sometimes I ponder life as a criminal,
ducking and diving, always outcast.
I suppose that such thoughts are merely subliminal
hints that life is galloping fast.

Sometimes I feel that I want to bulldoze
all of North London and live in a hut.
I suppose I had better get off to Waitrose,
pick up some supper before the shops shut.

THE ETERNAL TOOTHPASTE CONUNDRUM

I squeeze the toothpaste from the bottom,
carefully easing it up,
letting no morsel escape.
You squeeze the toothpaste from the middle.
some comes up,
some goes down,
which I
push
back up again.
Is this a symbol of our marriage?
An irresolvable conflict?
Or just the way we squeeze our toothpaste?
I don't know
and you
don't
care

HERE'S HOW I WANT IT

Spare me the double-breast pinstriped catafalque,
monochrome priest, scrag neck on dandruff shoulders,
intoning, droning, moaning his cold vicarage
and Tesco Basics suppers.

Spare me the mumbled hymns and high praise clichés,
no *Angels*, *My Way* or *I Will Always…*
Handcuff the organist, let no toccata
be sacrificed for me.

I want to hear those guitars soar,
the drum kit's roar and thumping bass,
ten thousand watts to shake the world
to wake it, make it know I've gone.

So put on your brightest clothes, my friends
and party, party, celebrate,
while I and dear old death, my pal
my constant chum for many years,
head for the pub
where there's no more
Time,
Gentlemen,
Please.

NO FLOWERS

I don't like flowers.
They're gaudy show-offs, pompous and floppy.
The lurid, neon daffodil and poppy
all make the place messy, they droop, they die
and each time they do, well, it seems, so do I.
No, I don't like flowers.

Please don't bring flowers.
Bring me dolly mixtures, Kinder Surprise,
a doll that opens and closes its eyes,
buy me bits of the moon, pieces of string,
chipolatas, organic fruit, any old thing
but, please, don't bring flowers.

She liked them, flowers.
I suppose you could say that they were her thing,
though to me they lie with their promise of spring.
She just had the knack, the touch, you see
of arranging them beautifully, unlike me.
So please, don't bring flowers.

TED

He was a rider of storms,
dancer in the midnight rain,
first into the autumn Cornwall sea,
Nessun Dorma bellowed
in the sleeping county town.

He was the laugh that roared out
over the crowded room,
bottle of wine on your doorstep
after a very bad week,
firm hand on the clifftop path.

It's a lot quieter and more peaceful now
but, as he would have said,
peace and quiet can be greatly overrated.

COUGH

I recognised my father by his cough,
a short sharp bark, parade ground rough.
The soldier's back, the rugby player's nose
were there but less specific, I suppose.
It would echo down the corridor when he was still way off,
that cough.

In his Georgian garden that terminal spring
as the coughs came more often and shook his paper skin,
we stood, divided by six feet and a life. Again
I threw my cheery banter at his parasitic pain
then in his pale blue eyes saw nothing
but the cough.

People often say they see or meet
dead friends, relations walking down the street.
Not me. I hear him in the pub's loud brawl,
at the rugby, in the evening in my hall,
the echo from my childhood, clear and sweet,
that cough.

CHANCE

In April '82 I missed my plane.
It crashed; some badly fastened hatch.
Not all were killed
but quite enough to show me how
a careless baggage handler at de Gaulle,
whom I had never met nor ever would,
had held my hour glass in his hand
and I knew nothing of it.

Since then I find it hard to plan
too far ahead.

Chance is a sometime friend
that dances in shadows,
trips the vain, then veers off laughing
till the next time he reminds us
that we're not here on our own.

'If only he, if only she,
what if and who'd have thought...'
We fend off, through banalities,
that casual flick of careless fingers,
sending us tacking far
from our well-charted shores.

And that's OK. Chance is not fate,
that poor excuse for inactivity.
Chance leaves us choice but taps us
on the shoulder now and then
and says 'Don't get too uppity,
my boy.' Then turns the page,
writes the first line of the chapter
that we did not know was there.

THE LAST HOT DAY

Chipping Ongar, Thaxted and Dunmow
sleep in the sun like contented cats,
while sharp shadows stretch on stubbled fields,
now shorn of their thrusting wheat.
And trees, whose leaves are travelling to gold,
shimmer to the light's orgasmic touch.

Three fields away, a tractor, like a sentry,
plods to and fro and birds that know
their journey's coming soon
swoop for sustaining grain.

In the town, the weightless light,
freed of the suppurating August haze,
throws knife-sharp patterns on the abbey floor.
The cold stone glows with pride,
once more a part of nature's deep eternity
as long ago, before the cutters'
chisel, axe and saw transformed it
from random lava to its current task,
footstool to a monumental God.

And, in the abbey gardens by the walls,
beer-bellied lads in cargo pants
kick balls and carry cans,
dance to the ice cream chimes,
while girls flirt and shout out mild obscenities.

The sun sinks. A silence falls.
All stand aware that many months will pass
and wars will come and go.
We'll celebrate and mourn,
give gifts, dream dreams and shiver
and the leaves will fall.

And then, one day, creeping in
coy, apologetic
like a cast-off lover,
the sun's heat once again
will stroke our aching souls.

WINTER BEACH

And the wind blows harsh
and the tide sweeps in and covers
the footsteps of the lovers
as they walk
cold
beneath the rusting stanchions
of the time-forgotten pier.

Above them, tired facades of upright houses,
Dunedin and Levershulme, Coombe Bay and Sailor's Rest
cling together, sodden soldiers
facing the machine gun rattle of November's gales.
Windows weep at the loss of light,
the greying of colour, triumph of the night.

And the caustic cries of the hovering birds
are stolen by the despot wind,
flung like gossip at the sulking town
where the lovers retreat,
hunkered down in the damp café.
She tucks wet hair behind her ear,
he watches his swirling coffee.
Both know what neither wants to say.

And the wind blows harsh
and the tide sweeps in and covers
the footsteps of the lovers.

WINDOW DREAMS

Saggy in sweatpants and grey bobbled fleece,
she stares through the fashion shop door,
sees herself swirling for one dreamy dance,
melting the young man's stuttering glance,
shining and carefree, just as before
on the warm sand of soft moon-kissed Greece.

Cashmere and silk then caressed her long legs
as she moved with a cat's purring grace.
But she knows in her heart she can't go there again
So, hunching her shoulders against the harsh rain
and brushing lank hair from a reddening face,
she walks on to Primark and Greggs.

GO WELL

Remember me,
not in those last hours
of hope and glasses shattered
in high decibel venom,
the whirlpool rages of no tomorrows
and tears of selfish reprimand.

Remember me rather in echoed hills,
whirling and swirling with the wind,
laughing through the pillow steam
of late night cafés
and dancing drunken on the silken beach.

When darkness dulls once vivid memories
and other voices drown our whispered love,
let me touch your arm, caress your midnight neck
and feel a welcome curving through your soul.

As time may pass, let no time pass at all
and please, remember me.

YOU SEE...

I meant to buy you flowers
really I did
I meant to tell you how nice your hair looked
how great you were at the party

I meant to tell you but the words got stuck
somewhere between a public school education
and all the crap that men are meant to be
I meant to
meant to
stuttered up
and wandered off into more comfortable worlds
of logic and analysis, sport and beer

I meant to
sorry
even that's a word that just can't struggle
past the gated censure of lips drawn tight
across a fearful heart
that longs to learn from yours
but dare not grasp
the rose thorn of emotion's blast

tell me I'm not lost
take me into dark entangled woods
and in that darkness let me see
the clear light I was meant to be

HANGING ON

Grey skies, grey cars
Grey men crouched over handlebars
Wipers slash at marauding rain
And he's hanging on by his fingertips.

ON THE TRAIN

You hide in sleep,
while frowning clouds and I
exchange dark glares through the silent window
and the flash, flash, flash of the telegraph poles
marks metronomic loss.

The morning squalls have ebbed
into the sullen sulk of Midlands midday grey;
drag-footed No Man's Land
where broken industry sentinels
stand guard, awaiting
orders long since lost.

I thought we were on our way to the sun
but, somewhere along the line,
one of us switched the points.
Now I feel our tracks diverge
beyond the reach of outstretched fingers,
already too late for a final touch.

We are only where we are,
travelling to, travelling from
going nowhere.

BOOKENDS

Desiccated by the uncaring sun,
they sit at the pavement café.
He stares to the North, she to the East,
both seeking coldness, ammunition
against the heat, against each other,

their silence a fortress,
heart-high, granite hard,
built by years of unspoken slights,
impenetrable, save the occasional glancing grunt,
unvalued, lost to the fetid air.

She wonders whether Jeffrey from accounts
might not have been a better bet,
in the long run.
He mourns the loss of trips to Frankfurt,
where expenses and anonymity
for one night eased the pain.

They sip their coffee,
watch the passers by,
and form unshared opinions.
She wonders whether she dares
take the crossword out of her bag.

WHEN THE FLU CAME

He was exiled to school on a windswept hill,
built to make men out of shapeless youth.
Dormitories smelled of dust and sweat,
ice in the washbasins, fear in the chapel,
beatings in every dark corner.

Not moulded to that place, he chose
subdued invisibility.
But still one older boy, half man,
sensing the fragile child,
pounded hope and home into taunting memories,
taught him fear.

In February, when the wind was coldest,
flu swept in from the East,
sucked the strength from strong young bodies,
capricious about who to spare
and who to take.

The young boy watched his persecutor felled,
saw him screaming, streaked in fear.
And as he watched he felt his world
regain its rhythm, click back into place.

Daylight came, the bed was coldly empty;
Word went round the college, 'Fyfield's died'.
Pale shocked faces whispered tears around him,
the boy was calm, believed in answered prayers.

When, next day, the bully's parents came -
he a civil servant, she a teacher -
in the quiet dignity of English grief,
mourning a memory alien to the boy's,
he frowned, frustrated that his purity of joy
be sullied by a complicating thought:
that this felled beast would be forever golden,
while he remained
one boy who didn't catch the flu.

THE GARDEN

When it's all over, Tilly,
when I get back home,
I'll take you to the garden
where we played when we were young.

I'll take you to the garden,
take you to our tree
that sighs and bends its beaten head
to the bustling autumn breeze,
spreading wide its barren arms
in welcome or farewell.

The flowers have all gone now, Tilly,
waiting underground,
hoping for another spring,
hoping for another spring.

When it's all over, Tilly,
when I get back home
I'll take you to the garden
and we'll play
just as before,
when we were young.

ACKNOWLEDGEMENTS

So many people in so many places have helped and guided me as I've found my feet. If I pick out a few, I miss the many, but some must be thanked.

Hill Slavid, Richard Cutler and everyone at the writing groups and at Herga Poets for their wise and constructive criticism; Siobhan Curham for advising me to stick to one thing; Mike Deller for pointing out clever things that I didn't know I'd done; Dorothy Pope for editing advice; Anjan Saha for getting me in front of a live audience and helping me to understand that my work communicates.

My thanks to Colin Robinson for the photography and design of the cover and to Carole Griffin for guidance on layout.